CONTENTS

4   Terrible lizards

6   All shapes and sizes

8   *Cryolophosaurus*

10   *Tuojiangosaurus*

12   *Deinonychus*

14   *Spinosaurus*

16   *Argentinosaurus*

18   *Struthiosaurus*

20   *Parasaurolophus*

22   *Therizinosaurus*

24   *Tyrannosaurus*

26   *Triceratops*

28   Timeline

30   Glossary

31   Further information

32   Index

TERRIBLE LIZARDS

Dinosaurs capture our imagination more than any other prehistoric animal. Their name means 'terrible lizard', and these prehistoric reptiles lived on Earth for more than 160 million years – at least 800 times longer than our own species has existed.

Dinosaurs arrive!

The first known dinosaurs appeared in what is now Argentina more than 230 million years ago (mya).* They were the small and speedy *Herrerasaurus* and *Eoraptor* – part of the theropod group that later included fearsome *Carcharodontosaurus* ('shark-toothed lizard') and *Tyrannosaurus rex* ('tyrant lizard king').

Triassic plant-eater

Plateosaurus lived in what is now northern Europe from around 214 mya. It was an ancestor of the huge, long-necked sauropods, but it walked on two legs instead of four.

∧ Plateosaurus
had leaf-shaped serrated teeth for tearing through plant foods.

*All the dates in this book are approximate.

PREHISTORIC LIFE

DINOSAURS

BY CLARE HIBBERT AND RUDOLF FARKAS

FRANKLIN WATTS

Franklin Watts
This paperback edition published in Great Britain in 2023 by Hodder & Stoughton
Copyright © Hodder & Stoughton, 2023

Credits
Series Editor: Amy Pimperton
Series Designer: Peter Scoulding
Picture Researcher: Diana Morris

Picture credits:
Linda Bucklin/Shutterstock: 7t, 7b.
Akkharat Jaruilawong/Shutterstock: 6.
Eva K/GFDL. CC-BY-SA/Wikimedia Commons: 4, 5b.
Eric Isselee/Shutterstock 5t.

HB ISBN 978 1 4451 5916 4
PB ISBN 978 1 4451 5917 1

Printed in China

Franklin Watts
An imprint of
Hachette Children's Group
Part of Hodder & Stoughton
Carmelite House
50 Victoria Embankment
London EC4Y 0DZ

An Hachette UK Company
www.hachettechildrens.co.uk

FSC
www.fsc.org
MIX
Paper from
responsible sources
FSC® C104740

Note to parents and teachers:
Every effort has been made by
the Publishers to ensure that the
websites in this book are suitable
for children, that they are of
the highest educational value,
and that they contain no
inappropriate or offensive
material. However, because of
the nature of the Internet, it is
impossible to guarantee that the
contents of these sites will not
be altered. We strongly advise
that Internet access is supervised
by a responsible adult.

This is the world's largest lizard – the Komodo dragon. Lizards' legs splay out from the sides of the body. Dinosaurs' legs were under the body.

The Mesozoic Era (252-66 mya) is known as the time when reptiles ruled Earth. Dinosaurs dominated on land, pterosaurs flew through the skies and the oceans were full of marine reptiles, such as plesiosaurs and ichthyosaurs.

Eoraptor was about the size of a pet cat. Its diet probably included insects and plants as well as meat.

ALL SHAPES AND SIZES

Dinosaurs ranged in size from tiny *Parvicursor*, barely bigger than a blackbird, to *Argentinosaurus*, the largest known land animal. There may have been smaller or larger ones, but we haven't found their fossils yet.

Written in stone

Fossils are bones and other remains – including footprints and eggs – that have been preserved in rock. By studying fossils, palaeontologists have pieced together a dinosaur family tree. There are two branches, based on the animals' hip bones. The saurischians had hips like modern lizards and were made up of the meat-eating theropods and plant-eating sauropods. The ornithiscians had hips like modern birds and included stegosaurs, ankylosaurs, hadrosaurs and ceratopsians.

Archaeopteryx *fossil* >

Bird-hipped dinosaurs, such as Stegosaurus, were all plant-eaters.

LIVING DINOSAURS

Birds are a type of feathered dinosaur that evolved from the theropods during the Jurassic Period. They survived when the non-avian (non-bird) dinosaurs were wiped out in a major extinction around 66 mya.

The feathered dinosaur Archaeopteryx is sometimes called the missing link between dinosaurs and modern birds. It shared features with both.

CRYOLOPHOSAURUS

PRONUNCIATION:	CRY-oh-loaf-oh-SAWR-us
CLADE:	Tetanurans
LIVED:	Early Jurassic Period, 194–188 mya
RANGE:	Antarctica
HABITAT:	Woodlands
WEIGHT:	465 kg (1,025 lb)
LENGTH:	6.5 m (21.3 ft)

Deadly carnivore *Cryolophosaurus* doesn't have a very serious nickname. It's known as Elvisaurus because its strange, forward-pointing crest resembles the hairstyle of the famous American rock-and-roll star, Elvis Presley.

Cryolophosaurus probably relied on its head decoration to impress females, just like today's crested lizards and birds. This dinosaur wasn't as big as later theropods, such as *Giganotosaurus*, but it was one of the Early Jurassic's largest predators, standing 1.6 m (5.2 ft) at the shoulder. *Cryolophosaurus* was the first meat-eating dinosaur to be discovered on Antarctica. Fossil hunting is a challenge there, because the ground is frozen.

JURASSIC HABITAT

Antarctica is an icy desert today, but 190 mya it was further north and closer to the equator. Thick forests grew in its moist, warm climate, but winters were cool with long hours of darkness.

This Cryolophosaurus has snatched a baby Glacialisaurus. Adult Glacialisauruses were too strong for Cryolophosaurus to overcome, weighing as much as 5.5 tonnes (6 tons).

TUOJIANGOSAURUS

PRONUNCIATION: TOO-yang-oh-SAWR-us
FAMILY: Stegosaurs
LIVED: Late Jurassic Period, 160 mya
RANGE: Sichuan Province, China
HABITAT: Woodlands
WEIGHT: 2.8 tonnes (3.1 tons)
LENGTH: 6.5 m (21.3 ft)

Named after *Stegosaurus*, all members of the stegosaur family had plates along their neck, back and tail, often in facing pairs. *Tuojiangosaurus*'s plates stopped halfway along the tail.

STAYING SAFE

If *Tuojiangosaurus* became separated from the herd, it could defend itself with a powerful swing of its spiked tail. The spikes stuck out at angles and were sharp enough to pierce an attacker's skin.

Stegosaur plates have puzzled palaeontologists over the years, but most now agree that they were used for display. The plates may have also helped the dinosaurs to keep their temperature steady, but weren't tough enough to act as armour. Like all stegosaurs, *Tuojiangosaurus* moved in a herd, feeding on low-lying vegetation. Sticking together meant each individual had less chance of being picked off by predatory theropods, such as *Yangchuanosaurus*.

Tuojiangosaurus is named after the Tuo River that flows through Sichuan, in southern China – the place where its fossils were found.

DEINONYCHUS

PRONUNCIATION:	dy-NON-ik-us
FAMILY:	Dromaeosaurs
LIVED:	Early Cretaceous Period, 115–108 mya
RANGE:	North America
HABITAT:	Swamps, floodplains
WEIGHT:	85 kg (187 lb)
LENGTH:	3.4 m (11.2 ft)

Wolf-sized *Deinonychus* hunted in packs so that it could take down prey that was much larger than itself. It probably lived in packs too, just like living wolves.

Like all members of the dromaeosaur family of feathered theropods, *Deinonychus* had a hooked claw on its extra-long second toe. This deadly, 13-cm-long (5 in) weapon gave the dinosaur its name, which means 'terrible claw'. One powerful slash could cause a victim to bleed to death. Claws were also useful for clinging on to prey. *Deinonychus* could bite harder than a hyena, but it mostly used its teeth to tear off flesh rather than chomp through bone.

FLUFFY FEATHERS

Feathers probably evolved from scuffed, frayed scales. Dinosaurs that had them stayed warmer because the fluffy down kept in heat. In time, feathers were used for showing off, too.

The hadrosaur Tenontosaurus weighed around 1.5 tonnes (1.7 tons). Deinonychus could only bring one down through teamwork.

SPINOSAURUS

PRONUNCIATION:	SPY-nuh-SAWR-us
FAMILY:	Spinosaurs
LIVED:	Cretaceous Period, 112–93.5 mya
RANGE:	North Africa
HABITAT:	Rivers, riverbanks, lakes, shores
WEIGHT:	9 tonnes (9.9 tons)
LENGTH:	16 m (52.5 ft)

Spinosaurus is the biggest carnivorous (meat-eating) dinosaur that we know about. Just its skull was a boggling 1.75 m (5.7 ft) long, which is large enough to hold a woman of average height.

Spinosaurus's skull was narrow and pointed, like a crocodile's. The position of the nostrils suggest that it spent a lot of time underwater like a crocodile, too. A row of long spines stuck up from *Spinosaurus*'s backbone and probably held a large sail of skin. This sail may have helped to soak up heat – or perhaps it shaded the water so *Spinosaurus* could see fish without being distracted by surface reflections.

BAD LUCK STORY

German palaeontologist Ernst Stromer (1870-1952) named *Spinosaurus* and found its first fossils in Egypt around 1912. Unfortunately, Stromer's specimens were destroyed during the Second World War (1939-45) in a bombing raid.

Spinosaurus hunted fish, crocodilians and land animals, including other dinosaurs.

ARGENTINOSAURUS

PRONUNCIATION:	AH-gen-teen-uh-SAWR-us
CLADE:	Titanosaurs
LIVED:	Late Cretaceous Period, 97–93.5 mya
RANGE:	Argentina
HABITAT:	Floodplains, forests
WEIGHT:	82 tonnes (90 tons)
LENGTH:	35 m (115 ft)

When a farmer found the first *Argentinosaurus* fossil – a leg bone – in 1987, he mistook it for a tree trunk! This record-breaking dinosaur needed broad, chunky legs to support its huge bulk.

Argentinosaurus weighed more than 12 large elephants. Titanosaurs are huge members of the long-necked, lumbering plant-eaters – the sauropods. When the herd stopped to feed, each individual could reach a wide area of vegetation from one spot, thanks to its long neck. This saved energy. Unlike meat, plants aren't a high-energy food. *Argentinosaurus* had to eat non-stop and keep moving on to find fresh supplies.

FROM EGG TO ADULT

A female *Argentinosaurus* laid more than ten eggs at a time, each the size of a rugby ball. Only a fraction of these hatched and made it to adulthood. It took 30 or 40 years for an *Argentinosaurus* to grow to full size.

Predators such as Giganotosaurus (below, right) circled Argentinosaurus' nesting sites, hoping to raid eggs or pick off hatchlings. ∨

STRUTHIOSAURUS

PRONUNCIATION:	STROO-thee-oh-SAWR-us
FAMILY:	Nodosaurs
LIVED:	Late Cretaceous Period, 85–66 mya
RANGE:	Northern Europe
HABITAT:	Woodlands
WEIGHT:	100 kg (220 lb)
LENGTH:	2.2 m (7.2 ft)

Struthiosaurus was one of the smallest armoured dinosaurs – it would have taken 70 of them to balance an *Ankylosaurus* on the scales. Its back was studded with bony plates called osteoderms and it also had shoulder spikes.

Each osteoderm had its own covering, called a scute, which was made of keratin – the tough material that forms our nails. As well as its longer shoulder spikes, *Struthiosaurus* had a row of shorter spikes along each side. This was typical of nodosaurs ('knobbed lizards'), which were a family of ankylosaurs without tail clubs. Other nodosaurs included *Sauropelta*, *Nodosaurus* and *Edmontonia*, which all lived in North America during the Cretaceous Period.

IS IT A BIRD?

The first person to examine *Struthiosaurus*, the 19th-century Austrian palaeontologist Emanuel Bunzel (1828-1895), didn't realise it was a dinosaur! Seeing it had a mix of bird and reptile features, he named the mysterious creature *Struthiosaurus* ('ostrich lizard').

Struthiosaurus fed on low-growing ferns, cycads (palm-like plants) and flowering plants.

PARASAUROLOPHUS

PRONUNCIATION:	pah-rah-SAWR-ol-uh-fes
FAMILY:	Hadrosaurs
LIVED:	Late Cretaceous Period, 83.5–70.6 mya
RANGE:	North America and possibly China
HABITAT:	Swamps, floodplains, forests
WEIGHT:	3 tonnes (3.3 tons)
LENGTH:	9.5 m (31 ft)

Parasaurolophus was one of the hadrosaurs – dinosaurs with flattened snouts that are sometimes known as the 'duck-bills'. Its name means 'like *Saurolophus*' and was chosen because of its similarity to another duck-billed dinosaur, *Saurolophus*.

TWO LEGS OR FOUR?

Parasaurolophus moved and grazed on all fours, but it stood on its hind legs to look around for danger. It could also run on two legs, reaching **40 kph (25 mph)** over short distances.

Parasaurolophus used its beak-like mouth to snip off leaves, grasses or horsetail stalks, which it chewed up with hundreds of tiny teeth. Like many hadrosaurs, it had a striking head crest for showing off, attracting a mate, seeing off a rival or simply recognising others in the herd. *Parasaurolophus*'s crest had another function, too – it was hollow, with tubes to and from the nose, and would have amplified its calls (made them louder).

Parasaurolophus's booming call might have been to sound the alarm or to attract a mate. >

THERIZINOSAURUS

PRONUNCIATION:	THAIR-uh-ZEEN-uh-SAWR-us
FAMILY:	Therizinosaurs
LIVED:	Late Cretaceous Period, 70 mya
RANGE:	Mongolia
HABITAT:	Swamps, floodplains
WEIGHT:	5 tonnes (5.5 tons)
LENGTH:	10 m (33 ft)

Therizinosaurus was an unusual theropod – even though it was armed with slasher claws, it wasn't a hunter. Its leaf-shaped teeth suited a diet of plants, and it also ate fungi, minibeasts and some small animals.

Therizinosaurus's 1-m-long (3.3 ft) claws could strip away tree bark to find grubs and sap, tear off vegetation or dig into termite nests. They also put off attackers such as *Tarbosaurus*, the Asian *T. rex*, which preferred to target prey that didn't have deadly 'scissorhands'. *Therizinosaurus* was the largest of the therizinosaurs, or 'scythe lizards'. The smallest was *Beipiaosaurus*, which was 2.2 m (7.2 ft) long and weighed just 85 kg (185 lb).

EMPTY SHELLS

In 2011, palaeontologists found the largest-known nesting colony of non-avian dinosaurs - 17 clutches of therizinosaur eggs in the Gobi Desert, Mongolia. The clutches contained a total of about 75 eggs, which all seemed to have hatched.

Most theropods had three toes and a small dewclaw, but Therizinosaurus stood on four toes.

Tyrannosaurus

PRONUNCIATION:	tye-RAN-uh-SAWR-us
FAMILY:	Tyrannosaurs
LIVED:	Late Cretaceous Period, 68–66 mya
RANGE:	North America
HABITAT:	Floodplains, swamps, forests
WEIGHT:	8.2 tonnes (9 tons)
LENGTH:	12 m (39 ft)

One species of tyrannosaur – *Tyrannosaurus rex*, or *T. rex* for short – is probably more famous than any other dinosaur. Until the discovery of *Spinosaurus*, it was the largest known land predator.

It's no longer the biggest, but *T. rex* is still a record-breaker, boasting a more powerful bite than any other land animal. Its jaw was 1.2 m (4 ft) long and contained up to 58 serrated teeth that could tear through flesh and crush bone. The largest of its teeth were 15 cm (6 in) long. *T. rex* hunted by stealth – it had a relatively large brain for a dinosaur (bigger than a basketball) and excellent senses.

SUPER SUE

Since *T. rex* was first described in 1905, more than 50 specimens have been found. The most complete, known as Sue, was found in 1990. Its well-preserved skull provided evidence of *T. rex*'s keen sight, smell and hearing.

V *This T. rex is creeping up on a pair of male* Pachycephalosauruses. *They are too busy flank-fighting to notice it!*

TRICERATOPS

PRONUNCIATION:	try-SERRA-tops
FAMILY:	Ceratopsians
LIVED:	Late Cretaceous Period, 68–66 mya
RANGE:	North America
HABITAT:	Floodplains, swamps, forests
WEIGHT:	8 tonnes (8.8 tons)
LENGTH:	8.5 m (28 ft)

With a pair of 1-m-long (3 ft) brow horns and a slightly shorter nose horn, *Triceratops* certainly deserved its name, which means 'three-horned face'. These weapons helped to defend against predators and to combat rivals.

Truck-sized *Triceratops* was one of the largest ceratopsians (dinosaurs with horned faces and a thick, bony 'frill' around the face), with a skull about 2 m (6.6 ft) long. Its size didn't put off Tyrannosaurs – some *Triceratops* fossils have tyrannosaur bite marks! *Triceratops* was a plant-eater with a beak-like mouth. It had 800 cheek teeth for grinding down cycads, palms and other tough plants. When, around 66 mya, dust blotted out the Sun and plants died, *Triceratops* couldn't survive.

WHAT HAPPENED?

Triceratops was one of the last non-avian dinosaurs. They died out 66 mya, along with other animal groups, including plesiosaurs and pterosaurs. Most scientists believe that the extinction was triggered by a huge meteorite (space rock) crashing into Earth.

Just like stags and other horned mammals today, Triceratops battled rival males by locking horns.

TIMELINE

This timeline shows the different periods, or chunks of time, since life began on Earth. It includes the appearance of key species in this book, as well as when some of them became extinct.*

Eon

Precambrian 4,600–541 mya	
3,600 mya	First life forms – bacteria

Era   Period

PALAEOZOIC 541–252 mya

Cambrian 541–485 mya	

Ordovician 485–443 mya	
455-430 mya	First major extinction wipes out 85 per cent of all species

Silurian 443–419 mya	

Devonian 419–359 mya	
400 mya	Ammonites, flying insects and land vertebrates appear
407–359 mya	Second major extinction wipes out 75 per cent of animal species, including all land vertebrates

Carboniferous 359–299 mya	
354 mya	Land vertebrates evolve again

Permian 299–252 mya	
266–252 mya	Third major extinction wipes out 95 per cent of marine species and 70 per cent of land species

* All the dates on these pages are approximate.

Era	Period		

MESOZOIC 252–66 mya

CENOZOIC 66 mya–TODAY

Triassic 252–201 mya

250 mya	Ichthyosaurs appear
245 mya	First dinosaurs
231 mya	*Herrerasaurus* and *Eoraptor*
215 mya	Pterosaurs and plesiosaurs appear
215–204 mya	*Plateosaurus*
201 mya	Fourth major extinction wipes out 76 per cent of all species

Jurassic 201–145 mya

194–188 mya	*Cryolophosaurus*
163.5–100.5 mya	*Stegosaurus*
160 mya	*Tuojiangosaurus*
150.8–148.5 mya	*Archaeopteryx*

Cretaceous 145–66 mya

115–108 mya	*Deinonychus*
112–93.5 mya	*Spinosaurus*
97–93.5 mya	*Argentinosaurus*
85–66 mya	*Struthiosaurus*
83.5–70.6 mya	*Parasaurolophus*
72 mya	*Parvicursor*
70 mya	*Therizinosaurus*
68–66 mya	*Tyrannosaurus* and *Triceratops*
66 mya	Fifth major extinction wipes out 80 per cent of animal species, including non-avian dinosaurs, pterosaurs, plesiosaurs and more

Palaeogene 66–23 mya

Neogene 23–2.6 mya

Quaternary 2.6 mya–today

200,000 years ago (ya)	Our species, *Homo sapiens*, appears in Africa

GLOSSARY

allosaur A large theropod with a long, narrow skull, usually with ornamental horns or crests

ancestor An earlier living organism that others are descended from

ankylosaur An ornithischian dinosaur with defensive osteoderms and, sometimes, a tail club

carnivore A meat-eater

climate The average weather of a place over a long period of time

dewclaw A small side toe that doesn't reach the ground and isn't a functioning part of the foot

dinosaur An extinct land reptile from the Triassic, Jurassic or Cretaceous periods, whose legs came straight down from its body rather than splaying out like a modern reptile's

dromaeosaur A small theropod with an outsize claw on each back foot

evolve To change from one species to another over millions of years, by passing on useful characteristics from one generation to the next

extinct Describes an animal or plant that has died out for ever

fossil The remains of a plant or animal that died long ago, preserved in rock

fungus One of a group of living things that feed on organic matter. Fungi include mushrooms, yeasts and moulds.

hadrosaur An ornithischian dinosaur with a beak-like mouth

ichthyosaur A dolphin-like, predatory marine reptile that lived in the Triassic, Jurassic and Cretaceous periods

marine Of or from the ocean

nodosaur An ankylosaur with bumps and spikes on its skull, but no tail club

non-avian Not from the Aves (modern birds) class of living things

ornithischian Having hip bones arranged like a modern bird's. Hadrosaurs, stegosaurs and ankylosaurs were all ornithischians.

osteoderm A lumpy scale on a reptile's skin

palaeontologist A scientist who studies fossils

plesiosaur Long-necked predatory marine reptiles that lived in the Triassic, Jurassic and Cretaceous periods

predator An animal that hunts other animals for food

prehistoric From the time before written records

prey An animal that is hunted by other animals for food

pterosaur Flying reptiles with wings made from skin stretched over a long fourth finger

saurischian Having hip bones arranged like a lizard's. Theropods and sauropods were saurischians.

sauropod A long-necked, plant-eating dinosaur that walked on all fours

scute A casing or sheath made of keratin

serrated Having a jagged, saw-like edge

species One particular type of living thing. Members of the same species look like each other and can reproduce together.

spinosaur A theropod with a long, narrow snout for eating fish

stegosaur An ornithischian dinosaur with defensive bony plates along its back

therizinosaur A large, plant-eating theropod with three huge claws on each hand

theropod A two-legged, saurischian dinosaur, usually a meat-eater, with sharp teeth and claws

titanosaur A huge sauropod with an extra-small head. Many species had bumpy scutes on their scales.

tyrannosaur A large theropod with a huge head and relatively small arms

FURTHER INFORMATION

Books:

Birth of the Dinosaurs by Michael Bright (Wayland, 2016)

Children's Dinosaur and Prehistoric Animal Encyclopedia by Douglas Palmer (QED, 2014)

Dinosaur Infosaurus (series) by Katie Woolley (Wayland, 2017)

Dinosaurs: A Children's Encyclopedia (DK, 2019)

The Kingfisher Dinosaur Encyclopedia by Michael Benton (Kingfisher, 2012)

Professor Pete's Prehistoric Animals (series) by David West (Franklin Watts, 2019)

Write On: Dinosaurs (series) by Clare Hibbert (Franklin Watts, 2016)

Websites:

www.natgeokids.com/uk/discover/animals/prehistoric-animals/meet-some-deadly-dinos/
National Geographic Kids' guide to dinosaurs

nhm.org/site/explore-exhibits/permanent-exhibits/dinosaur-hall
The Natural History Museum of Los Angeles's dinosaur collection, including three *T. rex* skeletons

www.prehistoric-wildlife.com
An A–Z guide to prehistoric creatures

Places:

Dinosaur Isle, Isle of Wight
The Dinosaur Museum, Dorset
National Museum, Cardiff
National Museum of Scotland, Edinburgh
Natural History Museum, London
Pitt-Rivers Museum, Oxford
Sedgewick Museum of Earth Sciences, Cambridge
Ulster Museum, Belfast

INDEX

ankylosaurs 6, 18
Archaeopteryx 6–7, 29
Argentinosaurus 6,
  16–17, 29

Beipiaosaurus 22
Bunzel, Emanuel 18

Carcharodontosaurus 4
ceratopsians 6, 26–27
claws 12, 22
Cretaceous Period
  12–27, 29
Cryolophosaurus 8–9, 29

Deinonychus 12–13, 29
dromaeosaurs 12–13

Eoraptor 4–5, 29

feathers 7, 12
fossils 4, 5, 6, 7, 8

Giganotosaurus 8, 17
Glacialisaurus 8–9

hadrosaurs 6, 12–13,
  20–21
Herrerasaurus 4, 29

ichthyosaurs 5, 29

Jurassic Period 7–11, 29

Komodo dragons 5

Mesozoic Era 5
meteorites 26

nodosaurs 18–19

ornithiscians 6
osteoderms 18

Pachycephalosaurus 24–25
palaeontologists 6
Parasaurolophus 20–21, 29
Parvicursor 6, 29
Plateosaurus 4, 29
plesiosaurs 5, 26, 29

saurischians 6
sauropods 4, 6, 16–17
Spinosaurus 14–15, 25, 29
stegosaurs 6–7, 10–11, 29
Stegosaurus 7, 10, 29
Stromer, Ernst 14
Struthiosaurus 18–19, 29

teeth 4, 12, 20, 22, 25, 26
Tenontosaurus 12–13
theropods 4–10, 12–13,
  22–23
therizinosaurs 22–23, 29
Therizinosaurus 22–23, 29
titanosaurs 16–17
Triceratops 26–27, 29
Tuojiangosaurus 10–11, 29
tyrannosaurs 24–26
Tyrannosaurus rex 4, 22,
  24–25, 29

Yangchuanosaurus 10